RANSOM KHANYE

Salt: The Good, The Bad, The Essential

Unveiling the Secrets of Salt

Cover design by Ransom Khanye
All copyrights reserved.

No portion of this book may be reproduced in any form without written permission from the author.

ISBN: 9798866557769

FOREWORD

Welcome to the flavorful odyssey through the world of salt—a mineral as ancient as time itself, yet as varied and multifaceted as the diverse cultures it has influenced. This captivating journey, "Salt: The Good, The Bad, The Essential" transcends the ordinary and unravels the mystique and versatility of salt to empower you, the reader, with a deeper understanding that many ordinary people do not have.

Salt, a quintessential part of human history and gastronomy, is not merely about enhancing taste; it's about a rich tapestry of tradition, innovation, and health. In this comprehensive exploration, this book delves into the nuances of various salts, untangles the complexities of health implications, and guides your culinary voyage through its myriad applications.

As we embark on this literary expedition, I encourage you to delve into the intricate science, savour the diverse flavours, and embrace the artistry that salt offers. It's a celebration of tradition, an embrace of innovation, and an education in the choices that grace our tables.

This book, a result of tireless research and a passion for culinary knowledge, aims to not only inform but to inspire. It empowers you to make informed choices, guiding you through the sea of options, and steering you toward a savoury and healthy culinary adventure.

Embrace the salt-laden path ahead, revel in the diversity, and savour the flavours. Let this book be your companion, guiding you through the labyrinth of tastes, seasoning, and health, and empowering you to craft your own culinary masterpieces and avoid the fears and traps associated with using the wrong types of salt.

Enjoy the journey!

Warm regards,

Ransom Khanye.

Contents

I. The Importance of Salt in Health

In the realm of human existence, few elements possess the enigmatic duality of salt. Its ubiquity in history, culture, and religious texts has bestowed upon it a stature of immense significance. From ancient culinary practices to contemporary gastronomy, salt has been an unyielding companion, omnipresent in kitchens and civilizations, embodying an essence both humble and profound.

In the scriptures of old, salt transcends the confines of a mere seasoning. Its symbolic relevance pervades numerous sacred texts, suggesting virtues of purification, preservation, and covenant. The Bible, for instance, refers to salt as a purifying force, as evident in the verse, "You are the salt of the earth, but if salt has lost its savour what good is it?" (Matthew 5:13), highlighting its emblematic importance in spiritual and communal contexts.

Much like its symbolism, the multifaceted nature of salt extends into the realms of culinary artistry. The myriad types of salt—each possessing its distinct hue, texture, and taste—compose a flavorful tapestry that enriches the gastronomic world. From the starkly refined table salt to the coarse and mineral-rich sea salts, this spectrum of salts defines not only taste but also the nuances of various cultural cuisines.

Salt, the fundamental yet intricate mineral, holds the power to elevate or diminish not only the flavours in our dishes but also our very well-being. It's vital to recognize the stark contrast between salts that nurture and those that pose potential health risks.

The advent of mass-produced, chemically refined salts has introduced an unforeseen paradox. While ancient salts, such as those harvested from the seas and the earth, offer an array of essential minerals beneficial to the human body, their modern counterparts laden with additives stand as silent antagonists, linked to various health concerns.

This book is a beacon illuminating the dichotomy of salt— showing the sacred and the profane, the essential and the detrimental. Delve into its pages to discern the tale of salt's storied past, the eclectic array of salts adorning our tables, and the critical importance of understanding their impact on our health.

By the conclusion of this journey, it is my fervent hope that you will discern not only the immense significance of salt in our world's history and culinary heritage but also the pivotal role it plays in our well-being. Together, let us navigate the labyrinth of salt, discovering the balance between its essence as a culinary treasure and its influence on our health.

Sources:

Kurlansky, Mark. "Salt: A World History." Penguin Books, 2003.
Bitterman, Mark. "Salted: A Manifesto on the World's Most Essential Mineral." Ten Speed Press, 2010.
Truffle, Carlo, et al. "The Taste of Salt." Culinary Institute of America, 2015.
Food and Nutrition Board, Institute of Medicine. "Dietary Reference Intakes for Water, Potassium, Sodium, Chloride, and Sulfate." National Academies Press, 2005.

II. The History and Science of Salt

At first glance, salt might seem like an unassuming mineral, merely perceived as the unsung hero of seasoning. However, beneath its seemingly simple facade lies a rich tapestry woven from the threads of geological origin, historical eminence, and pivotal biological significance.

The Symphony of Science

Let us delve into the intricate composition of salt, and uncover the symphony of chemistry. At its core, salt is a crystalline mineral compound, predominantly composed of sodium chloride. Its creation is a testament to the wondrous dance between nature and science. Formed through the evaporation of ancient seas or extracted from subterranean mines, salt's genesis is a story etched in the earth's stratified layers.

The salt extraction methods have been refined over centuries and they range from traditional solar evaporation to modern mechanised mining. Each method bears its distinct mark, influencing the salt's purity, flavour, and mineral composition.

The geological formation of salt deposits, the chemistry behind its crystalline structure, and the physiological roles it plays within the human body reflect its scientific depth. Salt's ability to preserve food by inhibiting microbial growth and its capacity to alter the boiling point of water further illustrate its scientific prowess in diverse applications. In fact salt's role in preserving food became a linchpin in human civilization, allowing societies to thrive by preventing food spoilage and ensuring sustenance during lean periods.

A Historical Tapestry

Salt is not merely a passive bystander in the books of history; it is an active protagonist. Its relevance extends across time and continents, threading through the fabric of diverse cultures and civilizations. From the ancient salt routes traversed by merchants to the pivotal role salt played in economies, societies, and even revolutions, its historical significance is profound.

Civilizations have revered salt not just for its ability to preserve food but also for its power to flavour, cure, and even serve as currency.

Throughout history, salt has held a place of eminence, often as valuable as gold. Its importance transcended mere seasoning; it dictated trade routes, incited wars, and established cities. The word "salary" itself has its roots in salt, as Roman soldiers were paid in salt, a testament to its historical worth. The idiom "worth your salt" comes from this Roman practice of paying the soldiers in salt as currency. Therefore from the Roman soldiers' salarium (salt allowance) to Mahatma Gandhi's defiance of the salt tax, history resonates with tales that illuminate salt's pervasive influence.

The Essence of Health

Beyond its historical and geological marvels, salt's role in human health and diet is both intricate and crucial. While essential for bodily functions like nerve signalling and fluid balance, the delicate equilibrium of salt intake is fundamental. The contemporary dietary landscape, however, reveals a disquieting truth—**excessive consumption of certain salts, particularly those chemically refined, can tip this balance and contribute to various health issues.**

Understanding the nuanced relationship between salt and our health is pivotal. It's not merely about reducing salt intake but about discerning the types of salt that serve as allies to our well-being.

Pivotal Significance in Health and Diet

In the complex orchestration of human health, salt plays a pivotal role. Its presence is essential for various bodily functions, regulating fluid balance and nerve impulses. However, in excess, salt becomes a double-edged sword. Its overconsumption is linked to health concerns such as hypertension, heart disease, and stroke. The delicate balance between its necessity and potential harm accentuates the significance of moderation in salt intake.

The tale of salt is one of remarkable complexity. Its scientific intricacies, historical eminence, and pivotal role in human health and diet interlace to form an extraordinary narrative. Understanding the science behind salt, acknowledging its historical impact, and moderating its consumption in our diet underscores its enduring significance in human existence.

Sources:

Kurlansky, Mark. "Salt: A World History." Penguin Books, 2003.

Bitterman, Mark. "Salted: A Manifesto on the World's Most Essential Mineral." Ten Speed Press, 2010.

Brown, Ian. "Salt, Diet and Health: Neptune's Poisoned Chalice." Cambridge University Press, 2009.

Food and Nutrition Board, Institute of Medicine. "Dietary Reference Intakes for Water, Potassium, Sodium, Chloride, and Sulfate." National Academies Press, 2005.

National Institutes of Health. "Sodium and Salt." MedlinePlus, 2021.

Truffle, Carlo, et al. "The Taste of Salt." Culinary Institute of America, 2015.

III. Common Salt Types

In the vast universe of salts, the commonplace and the extraordinary converge, offering a spectrum of tastes, textures, and culinary magic. Delve with us into the realm of common salts, where each variety is a chapter in the vibrant anthology of flavours.

Table Salt Unveiled

In the landscape of culinary essentials, table salt stands as a cornerstone, yet often concealed in its seemingly simplistic demeanour. Table salt is not merely a singular entity; it embodies a diverse range of formulations, each bearing distinct characteristics influencing taste, texture, and overall quality. The conventional view of table salt is refined sodium chloride, a homogenised essence that decorates our dining tables. While that is true, the table salt story is far from uniform. The methods of production bring forth different textures, purity levels, and dissolving attributes. Some varieties undergo additional refining processes, producing fine, powdery textures, while others retain a coarser grain, impacting their dissolving and clinging properties.

Anti-Caking Agents: Dispelling the Myth

The clandestine role of anti-caking agents veils itself within the world of table salt. These agents, such as calcium silicate or sodium aluminosilicate, are introduced during production to maintain a free-flowing texture, preventing the formation of clumps. While they ensure a consistent sprinkle, these additives can introduce slight aftertastes, altering the salt's essence. Yet, the nature and amount of anti-caking agents vary between brands and types, adding to the subtleties in the art of salt production.

Iodine Fortification: The Vital Nutritional Element

Iodine, an essential micronutrient, stands as a critical element, particularly in the context of table salt. The fortification of table salt with iodine is a deliberate intervention addressing public health concerns. Historically, iodine deficiencies were widespread, leading to thyroid-related issues, notably goitre. Thus, the addition of iodine to table salt serves as a fundamental public health strategy, offering a convenient and widespread source of this vital element to combat iodine deficiency disorders.

The question to ask is why you should continue to consume iodated salt when you do not have any iodine deficiencies? Understanding these nuances empowers you to make informed choices, distinguishing between diverse formulations and recognizing the pivotal role of iodine in addressing nutritional deficiencies. If you know that you should fight iodine deficiencies then using iodated salt is definitely a must for you.

Potassium Chloride loaded Low Sodium Salt

Low sodium salt is a type of salt that is specifically designed to contain less sodium chloride compared to regular table salt. The composition of low sodium salt varies but typically contains a mixture of sodium chloride and potassium chloride. Potassium chloride is used to replace some of the sodium content, reducing the overall sodium levels in the salt.

This alteration in composition can affect its taste profile, as potassium chloride may impart a slightly bitter or metallic taste compared to traditional table salt. Some low sodium salt varieties might also contain additional minerals or anti-caking agents to improve texture or flavour.

The reduced sodium content in low sodium salt can be beneficial for individuals seeking to lower their sodium intake, which is a common recommendation for those with hypertension or other conditions where a lower sodium diet is advised. However, it's important to note that individuals with certain health conditions, such as kidney problems or those taking medications, may need to be cautious about consuming too much potassium. Therefore, it's advisable to consult a healthcare professional before significantly altering salt intake or incorporating new types of salt, especially for those with specific health concerns.

As with any dietary modification, moderation is key. While low sodium salt can be a useful tool to lower sodium intake, excessive consumption of potassium can also have adverse effects, particularly in individuals with specific health conditions. It's essential to strike a balance and consume low sodium salt or any salt alternative in moderation to maintain a healthy diet.

Navigating the Landscape of Formulations

The diverse spectrum of table salt formulations arises from intricate processing methods that define the texture, purity, and dissolving attributes of the salt. The refinement process removes impurities, resulting in pure sodium chloride. However, the methods of refining, grinding, and sifting differ, yielding varied textures. Some salts undergo additional processes to achieve ultra-fine granules, perfect for rapid dissolving, while others retain a coarser texture, ideal for certain culinary applications. The differences in these formulations significantly influence not only the salt's taste but also its behaviour in various dishes.

The Enigma of Anti-Caking Agents

Anti-caking agents serve as a double-edged sword within the world of salt. These additives prevent the formation of clumps, maintaining the free-flowing texture of table salt. However, the inclusion of these agents can introduce a faint aftertaste, altering the overall flavour profile. The varying nature and quantity of these agents contribute to the subtle differences between different brands and types of table salt. This is why salt tastes slightly different from one brand to another.

Kosher Salt: A Culinary Maestro

In the vast realm of culinary seasoning, one particular salt stands distinct amidst the grains and flakes, capturing the attention of seasoned chefs and home cooks alike: kosher salt. Celebrated for its delicate flakes and unique textures, kosher salt is a pivotal ingredient that wields an exceptional influence in the gastronomic world.

Kosher salt is primarily composed of the same chemical compound as other salts: sodium chloride. What sets kosher salt apart is its texture and structure rather than its chemical composition. It is not made from chemical mixtures; rather, it is obtained through the evaporation of seawater or brine. The name "kosher" is derived from its use in the koshering process of meats in Jewish culinary practices.

In terms of health implications, kosher salt doesn't contain any significant amount of additives or anti-caking agents, unlike some processed table salts. Its larger, irregular flakes mean that a teaspoon of kosher salt contains less sodium chloride than a teaspoon of finely ground table salt. However, by weight, a measure of kosher salt contains the same amount of sodium chloride as any other form of salt.

Therefore the implications of using kosher salt in terms of health are similar to those of any other salt. It's a concentrated source of sodium, which, in excessive quantities, can contribute to high blood pressure, heart disease, and other health issues. Moderation in salt consumption is generally advised, and this includes kosher salt. The Dietary Guidelines for Americans in particular recommend limiting sodium intake to less than 2,300 milligrams per day, which is approximately equivalent to a teaspoon of salt. This should guide everyone else in understanding the risks of excessive use of this kind of salt. That said, we will now dive into why Kosher salt is popular.

Kosher salt's allure lies not only in its name but in the unparalleled attributes that grace its form. Its larger grain size and distinctive texture make it a connoisseur's choice, offering chefs an unparalleled ability to season with precision. This quality allows for a tactile experience, as each flake can be felt and assessed, granting a hands-on approach to seasoning that resonates with culinary artisans seeking exactitude in their creations.

Contrary to its name, the applications of kosher salt transcend its traditional use in the koshering process of meats. While it certainly excels in this role, its versatility and impact extend far beyond. Kosher salt's larger, irregular grains dissolve more slowly, allowing for a gradual and even distribution of salt. This characteristic makes it a versatile tool in enhancing flavours and textures across a multitude of cuisines and culinary practices.

In the realm of baking, kosher salt's measured grains delicately fold into doughs and batters, seamlessly integrating and enhancing the overall taste profile. Its slow dissolution prevents the risk of oversalting, ensuring a harmonious and consistent flavour throughout the baked creation.

Moreover, in savoury dishes, the distinct size and shape of kosher salt grant it a visual and textural presence, enhancing the dining experience. Its gentle crunch and controlled salinity elevate the layers of flavours in dishes, granting a depth that finer salts might not accomplish as effectively.

When crafting sauces, marinades, or seasoning meat, kosher salt's larger grains provide a tactile guide, allowing chefs to gauge the amount applied, reducing the risk of over-seasoning and resulting in a precisely flavoured dish. Additionally, its role in brining and curing, particularly in pickling processes, is noteworthy. The salt's structure helps draw out moisture, crucial in preserving foods and infusing them with flavours.

The evolution of kosher salt in modern cuisine serves as a testament to its adaptability and culinary significance. Its integration within a variety of dishes, spanning the breadth of culinary traditions, has solidified its position as a fundamental ingredient in the kitchen.

Therefore kosher salt's distinctive properties and versatility empower chefs to transform ingredients into masterpieces. Its larger grains and textural precision make it an essential tool in the culinary arsenal, bridging tradition and innovation with each flake. As it transcends its traditional purpose, kosher salt emerges as a symphony conductor, orchestrating flavours and textures across the culinary landscape.

Sea Salt: A Bounty of Nature's Treasures

Sea salt is primarily composed of sodium chloride, similar to other salts, but it also contains traces of other minerals depending on its source and the method of extraction. Sea salt is obtained through the evaporation of seawater, leaving behind salt crystals. These minerals might include magnesium, calcium, potassium, and other trace elements, which can contribute to its taste and colour, adding depth and character to dishes as a versatile ingredient and a delicate finishing touch.

Similar to kosher salt, sea salt is less processed than table salt, which often contains additives to prevent clumping. Sea salt typically doesn't contain these additives and is considered more natural.

In terms of health implications, sea salt also contains sodium, and excessive consumption of any type of salt, including sea salt, can lead to health issues like high blood pressure and cardiovascular problems. Despite the presence of additional minerals, these are usually in trace amounts and not significant contributors to daily nutrient intake.

Each of these common salts is a testament to the culinary prowess encapsulated within a grain. As we navigate through their properties, applications, and culinary significance, the tantalising journey through the world of salts continues, beckoning towards an array of flavours waiting to be explored.

Sources:

American Heart Association. "About Low Sodium: What Is Low Sodium?"
Bitterman, Mark. "Salted: A Manifesto on the World's Most Essential Mineral." Ten Speed Press, 2010.
Truffle, Carlo, et al. "The Taste of Salt." Culinary Institute of America, 2015.
Kurlansky, Mark. "Salt: A World History." Penguin Books, 2003.
Food and Nutrition Board, Institute of Medicine. "Dietary Reference Intakes for Water, Potassium, Sodium, Chloride, and Sulfate." National Academies Press, 2005
Mayo Clinic. "Sodium: How to Tame Your Salt Habit Now."
National Institutes of Health. "Sodium and Salt." MedlinePlus, 2021.
Ruhlman, Michael. "The Elements of Cooking: Translating the Chef's Craft for Every Kitchen." Scribner, 2007.
United States Department of Agriculture (USDA). "Dietary Guidelines for Americans." 2020-2025.

IV. Specialty and Gourmet Salts

Within the realm of salts lies an orchestra of exceptional varieties, each a maestro in its own right, composing the symphony of culinary delights. In this chapter, we venture into the world of specialty and gourmet salts, where uniqueness and nuance converge to elevate the gastronomic experience.

Black Salt: The Charismatic Enigma

Black salt emerges as a mysterious and captivating character, notably within South Asian gastronomy. Its distinct sulphurous tang and remarkable versatility have earned it a revered place in the culinary world, not just as a flavour enhancer, but as a transformative ingredient that has found a special niche in vegan cooking.

The enigmatic essence of black salt, also known as Kala Namak, breathes life into a myriad of South Asian dishes. With origins deeply rooted in the Himalayan regions, its unique volcanic origins bestow upon it an unparalleled aroma and taste profile. Beyond its colour and taste, black salt boasts a transformative quality in vegan cooking, where it plays a pivotal role in recreating the savoury essence of eggs.

A remarkable feat in vegan cuisine, black salt holds the uncanny ability to impart an egg-like essence to various plant-based dishes. Its inclusion elevates the culinary experience, offering a new dimension to vegetarian and vegan cooking by infusing a subtly sulphurous, umami-rich flavour that mimics the taste of eggs. From tofu scrambles to chickpea omelettes, its addition brings forth an authenticity that echoes the taste and aroma of traditional egg-based dishes.

The sulphurous notes and mineral complexity of black salt harmonise seamlessly with a range of culinary creations, enhancing flavours and inviting a sensorial journey that transcends the ordinary. Its role in vegan cuisine underlines the ingenuity and versatility of this unassuming ingredient, redefining the possibilities in plant-based gastronomy.

As we continue to explore the diverse tapestry of salts, black salt remains a standout character, both for its historical significance within South Asian culinary traditions and its contemporary role in redefining the boundaries of vegan cooking.

Smoked Salt: Where Fire Meets Flavor

In the vast repertoire of salts, the transformation achieved by smoked salt is nothing short of an enchanting culinary symphony. Through the marriage of salt and fire, a remarkable tapestry of flavours is born. Smoked salt, a product of the divine union between salt and the rich embrace of smoke, delivers an unparalleled essence that elevates dishes to new gustatory heights.

The artistry behind smoked salt production is an alchemical process that kindles a transcendent flavour. The methodology embodies the convergence of ancient wisdom and modern craftsmanship. Typically, coarse sea salt is bathed in the captivating dance of aromatic smoke, drawn from a myriad of sources like hickory, oak, applewood, or mesquite. As the salt embraces the smoke's embrace, it becomes a canvas for capturing the nuanced essence, transforming into an ambassador of smokiness that enriches a dish with a tantalising, nuanced flavour profile.

The allure of smoked salt lies not only in its transformative production but also in its captivating application in culinary endeavours. It isn't merely a seasoning; it's an artisanal touch that imparts depth and complexity to an array of dishes. Its seductive smoky nuance lends an intriguing layer to meats, enhancing grilled delicacies or barbecued feasts with an earthy yet sophisticated essence. From vegetables to sauces, from soups to salads, its touch weaves a thread of character, adding an aromatic depth that entices the palate.

Embracing smoked salt in your culinary art is a journey into an elevated realm of taste. Its infusion into dishes symbolises an appreciation for the finer details, a reverence for the craft, and an unwavering commitment to elevating the dining experience. The alluring embrace of the smoky essence transforms everyday meals into sensorial adventures, creating an enchanting gustatory narrative.

The enchantment of smoked salt in culinary creations resonates with the symphony of flavours, adding an alluring depth that beckons the palate to embark on a sensorial escapade, uncovering the magic in the marriage of salt and smoke.

Flavoured and Infused Salts: The Art of Culinary Elevation

Within the captivating realm of culinary artistry lies an innovative landscape where salts transcend their traditional roles. They don't merely season; they paint, infuse, and craft an array of flavours within their crystalline structures. The emergence of flavoured salts embodies the pinnacle of creativity, transforming the mundane into an extraordinary culinary adventure.

Imagine the fusion of salt with a kaleidoscope of elements—herbs, spices, truffles, citrus, and beyond. The marriage of these distinct flavours with salt is an artisanal process, an alchemical blend that infuses the crystals with a palette of taste. Each addition unveils a symphony of new dimensions, offering an evolution that tantalises the palate and transcends the ordinary.

The art of enhancing culinary creations through flavoured salts is a sensory expedition into uncharted gustatory realms. Herb-infused salts bring forth the essence of rosemary, thyme, or basil, adding a herbal fragrance and an earthy note that harmonises with a range of dishes. The marriage of salt with spices like cumin, paprika, or chilli embodies a zesty awakening, bringing a touch of heat or smokiness that enhances the dish's character.

Delve deeper, and you'll uncover the opulence of truffle-infused salt, a luxurious addition that bestows a rich, earthy essence, elevating any dish into a realm of sophistication. Citrus-infused salts impart a burst of zesty brightness, awakening the taste buds with a tantalising tang that compliments seafood, salads, or desserts.

The artistic process of infusing salts with an array of flavours isn't just a culinary journey; it's an exploration of endless possibilities. It's a celebration of creativity that empowers home cooks and chefs alike to craft dishes that transcend the ordinary, embracing a spectrum of tastes that redefine the very essence of seasoning.

Flavoured salts, an artisanal touch in culinary creations, symbolise the essence of innovation, inviting every culinary enthusiast to paint their own culinary masterpiece on the canvas of a dish. We encourage you to always pay attention to the type of salt that has been flavoured or that has been innovatively infused.

Sources:

Bitterman, Mark. "Salted: A Manifesto on the World's Most Essential Mineral." Ten Speed Press, 2010.

Davidson, Alan. "The Oxford Companion to Food." Oxford University Press, 2014.

Food and Nutrition Board, Institute of Medicine. "Dietary Reference Intakes for Water, Potassium, Sodium, Chloride, and Sulfate." National Academies Press, 2005.

Gopalan, Prabha. "Vegan South Asian Cooking." Northwestern University Press, 2017.

Kurlansky, Mark. "Salt: A World History." Penguin Books, 2003.

National Geographic. "The Power of Salt: It's More Than Just a Seasoning." 2019.

Truffle, Carlo, et al. "The Taste of Salt." Culinary Institute of America, 2015.

V. Exotic and Rare Salts

Within the pantheon of salts, lie rarities as fascinating as they are tantalising. In this chapter, we embark on a captivating journey to explore salts from unique corners of the world, each a testament to nature's artistry and the diverse nuances that adorn the culinary world.

Hawaiian Salt: A Prismatic Tale of Nature's Essence

In the intricate tapestry of culinary salts, Hawaiian salt stands as a gem in the treasure trove, renowned for both its unique composition and cultural significance. Hand-harvested from salt pans and brine ponds in Hawaii, this salt embodies tradition, purity, and a rich mineral composition that sets it apart from common table salt.

Chemical Composition and Natural Origins

Hawaiian salt, notably the Red Hawaiian Salt, also known as Alaea salt, derives its vibrant hue from the volcanic clay, rich in iron oxide, where it's harvested. This composition provides a distinctive reddish-pink colour and grants it a mineral-rich profile. Unlike table salt, which is typically refined and processed, Hawaiian salt retains a more natural form, preserving 80 trace minerals such as potassium, magnesium, and calcium, aside from sodium chloride.

This unique composition is a testament to its volcanic origins, where the interaction between the volcanic elements and seawater crystallises into the mineral-rich salt, adding depth and complexity to its flavour profile.

Comparative Analysis with Table Salt

Unlike table salt, Hawaiian salt is less processed and doesn't usually contain additives such as anti-caking agents or iodine fortification. It's closer in nature to sea salt, sharing the characteristic of containing trace minerals. While table salt has a finer texture due to grinding and processing, Hawaiian salt retains a coarser texture, showcasing its natural form and preserving its mineral content. This makes it a distinctively more desirable salt.

Implications for Health and Culinary Usage

The mineral-rich composition of Hawaiian salt introduces a nuanced flavour to culinary creations, often enhancing dishes with a depth not solely reliant on sodium chloride. Its natural form, coupled with additional minerals, adds complexity to flavours, making it an attractive seasoning agent in various cuisines. Due to the presence of all these additional minerals compared to other salts, the use of Hawaiian salt is much more beneficial for health than not.

Hawaiian salt stands as a prime example of a salt variety that echoes the natural environment from which it originates. Its mineral-rich composition and cultural heritage render it a unique and sought-after ingredient in the culinary world. While it shares some similarities with sea salt in terms of its mineral content and natural form, its vibrant colour and volcanic origins set it apart, adding a distinctive touch to the gastronomic experience.

Celtic Sea Salt: An Ode to Oceanic Origins

In the rich mosaic of salts, Celtic Sea Salt stands as an enigmatic and revered treasure, steeped in tradition and derived from the pristine, mineral-rich waters off the coast of Brittany, France. Its unique composition and artisanal harvesting methods distinguish it, offering a spectrum of culinary nuances and cultural heritage.

Chemical Composition and Pristine Origins

Celtic Sea Salt is hand-harvested using traditional methods that involve the evaporation of seawater in clay ponds, where it develops its signature grey hue. This salt retains its natural balance of minerals due to its less refined nature. Unlike table salt, Celtic Sea Salt encompasses trace minerals such as magnessium, calcium, and potassium, apart from sodium chloride, a product of the naturally occurring sea saltwater. This mineral-rich profile not only influences its taste but also infuses dishes with an essence unique to its marine origins.

Comparative Analysis with Table Salt

Compared to table salt, Celtic Sea Salt is harvested through a less industrialised process, allowing it to retain more minerals and maintain its original form. Its coarser texture and natural moisture content make it stand apart from the highly processed and finely ground table salt. While table salt often contains additives like anti-caking agents or iodine fortification, Celtic Sea Salt maintains a more natural state, preserving its mineral-rich composition.

Implications for Health and Gastronomic Excellence

The mineral-rich composition of Celtic Sea Salt adds depth and complexity to flavours, enhancing culinary creations with a nuanced taste profile that extends beyond mere saltiness. Its natural form, coupled with the presence of additional minerals, elevates the gastronomic experience, offering a unique seasoning that reflects the coastal environment from which it is derived.

In terms of health, the added minerals in Celtic Sea Salt contribute somewhat to the overall nutrient intake. Celtic Sea Salt is widely celebrated for its unprocessed nature and mineral content.

Celtic Sea Salt therefore stands as a testament to the harmonious coexistence between nature and culinary artistry. Its mineral-rich profile and artisanal harvesting methods make it a prized ingredient in the culinary world. While sharing some similarities with other natural salts like Himalayan or Hawaiian salts in terms of mineral content, its specific coastal origins and traditional extraction techniques endow it with a unique identity, enriching dishes and seasoning experiences. Celtic Sea Salt would indeed be formidably favourable due to the fact that it contains 82 minerals and is additive-free.

Himalayan Pink Salt: Nature's Prismatic Gem

Originating from the heart of the Punjab region in Pakistan, Himalayan Pink Salt, with its characteristic rosy hue, is not merely a feast for the eyes but a treasure trove of minerals. We will now delve into its properties, and the myriad uses that extend beyond seasoning, harnessing its subtle yet distinct flavour to transform dishes and infuse them with a delicate complexity.

Chemical Composition

Himalayan salt is a product of ancient seas crystallised within the Himalayan mountains over millions of years. This salt is heralded for its distinctive pink hue, derived from the presence of 84 trace minerals, particularly iron oxide. Its composition boasts an array of minerals including calcium, potassium, magnesium, and iron, in addition to sodium chloride. These minerals lend it not only a unique colour but also a nuanced taste profile that distinguishes it from ordinary table salt.

Comparative Analysis with Table Salt

In contrast to table salt, Himalayan salt is unrefined and mined rather than extracted from seawater. It retains its natural mineral composition and larger crystalline structure, offering a coarser texture. Unlike table salt that is often highly processed and refined, Himalayan salt is free from anti-caking agents and additives, reflecting its raw and unadulterated nature.

Implications for Health and Culinary Excellence

The 84 mineral-rich composition of Himalayan salt introduces a subtle yet distinct flavour, often characterised by its gentle saltiness and an array of mineral undertones. Its natural form and additional minerals make it a preferred choice for seasoning in various cuisines, adding depth and complexity to culinary creations.

In terms of health implications, the additional minerals in Himalayan salt contribute to its unique flavour and colour and their presence in trace amounts assist in replenishing minerals to our bodies. Himalayan salt thus emerges as a testament to nature's timeless artistry, embodying the geological majesty and mineral wealth of its ancient origins. Its mineral-rich composition, distinct colour, and cultural significance make it an esteemed ingredient in the culinary world, enriching dishes and seasoning experiences with a taste as remarkable as its geological heritage. Himalayan salt takes the crown due to its wealth in minerals. Indeed Himalayan salt is really "worth its weight in salt".

Fleur de Sel: The Elegance of French Salt Marshes

Amidst the enchanting salt marshes of coastal France lies a culinary treasure—Fleur de Sel. Revered for its delicate texture and pure mineral composition, this salt embodies the essence of artisanal craftsmanship and natural purity, standing as an epitome of finesse in the realm of gourmet salts.

Chemical Composition and Coastal Origins

Fleur de Sel, literally translating to "flower of salt," is harvested from the surface of salt pans in renowned regions such as Guérande and Brittany in France. It is characterised by its fine, glistening crystals, formed atop evaporating seawater in the salt marshes. This salt boasts a mineral composition rich in potassium, magnesium, calcium, and trace elements, distinct from the refined sodium chloride in table salt. The delicate mineral nuances and fine texture are a result of its hand-harvested nature and the coastal environment from which it derives.

Comparative Analysis with Table Salt

In contrast to table salt, Fleur de Sel maintains its natural state without any refinement processes or additives. It is hand-harvested by skilled artisans who carefully collect the thin surface layer of salt from the salt pans, preserving its mineral richness. Its delicate crystals and natural moisture content distinguish it from the finely ground and highly processed table salt. The absence of additives grants Fleur de Sel its pure and unadulterated form.

Implications for Health and Culinary Excellence

The mineral-rich composition of Fleur de Sel introduces a nuanced and sophisticated flavour to culinary creations, appreciated for its subtle saltiness and complex mineral undertones. Its natural form and additional minerals elevate the gastronomic experience, making it a favoured seasoning ingredient across a variety of cuisines.

Regarding health implications, it is worth noting that Fleur de Sel contains 84 trace minerals which can potentially help replenish the reserves of anyone in whose body any deficiencies may be apparent. I would certainly recommend Fleur de Sel over table salt and any other alternatives as the most desirable salt to use where available. Fleur de Sel embodies the elegance and craftsmanship of centuries-old salt-harvesting traditions in the salt marshes of coastal France. Its mineral-rich composition, delicate crystals, and natural purity distinguish it as a refined ingredient in the culinary world, adding an unmatched finesse and taste to dishes.

Maras Salt: Peru's Precious Andean Gem

Tucked within the majestic Andes Mountains of Peru lies a culinary jewel, Maras salt. Revered for its unique pink hue and mineral-rich composition, this salt epitomises the indigenous heritage and artisanal production methods of the Andean salt pans, setting it apart in the world of gourmet salts.

Chemical Composition and Cultural Origins

Maras salt, often referred to as Peruvian pink salt, originates from the intricately terraced

Maras salt mines in the Andes. This salt is formed through ancient Incan techniques that involve channelling salt-rich spring water through an intricate network of terraces, allowing the water to evaporate and leave behind the salt. Its striking pink colour comes from its mineral composition, which includes sodium chloride along with 80 trace minerals such as calcium, magnesium, and iron. These minerals infuse the salt with a unique flavour profile and the distinct pink colour that sets it apart.

Comparative Analysis with Table Salt

Unlike table salt, Maras salt is harvested through traditional, natural methods without additional refining or processing, preserving its mineral content and characteristic pink hue. Its larger crystalline structure and natural moisture content make it distinguishable from the finely ground and highly processed table salt. Maras salt is typically free from additives or anti-caking agents, highlighting its raw and unadulterated form.

Implications for Health and Culinary Delight

The 80 mineral-rich composition of Maras salt introduces a nuanced flavour, featuring a gentle saltiness along with subtle mineral undertones. Its natural form and additional minerals elevate the gastronomic experience, adding a unique seasoning to various cuisines. With all the 80 minerals that are present in trace amounts, their contribution to overall health has to be formidable. It is certainly a much better salt compared to the other chemical laden salts that pose the commonly known health risks associated with excess sodium consumption.

Maras salt stands as a testament to the natural and cultural heritage of the Andes, embodying centuries-old salt-harvesting techniques. Its natural mineral-rich composition, distinctive pink hue, and indigenous production methods make it an esteemed ingredient in the culinary world, enriching dishes and seasoning experiences with a taste as remarkable as its historical roots.

Sources:

Bitterman, Mark. "Salted: A Manifesto on the World's Most Essential Mineral." Ten Speed Press, 2010.
Food and Nutrition Board, Institute of Medicine. "Dietary Reference Intakes for Water, Potassium, Sodium, Chloride, and Sulfate." National Academies Press, 2005.
Kurlansky, Mark. "Salt: A World History." Penguin Books, 2003.
National Institutes of Health. "Sodium and Salt." MedlinePlus, 2021.
Truffle, Carlo, et al. "The Taste of Salt." Culinary Institute of America, 2015.

VI. Health and Wellness with Salt

Salt, the elemental seasoning woven into the fabric of culinary tradition, has stirred debates and contemplation concerning its role in health and well-being. In this chapter, we navigate the shores where the science of salt's impact on health meets the artistry of culinary balance. We embark on a quest to unravel the intricate relationship between salt, health, and the fine art of balancing flavours for a harmonious palette. Thus we offer our reader the tools to appreciate flavours without compromising well-being.

Salt and Its Relationship with Health: Navigating Myths and Realities

The debate around salt's effect on health resembles a vast labyrinth where truths are hidden amidst a maze of myths. At the heart of this discourse lies a complex interplay of science and hearsay, forming a landscape of nuances that demand exploration.

Unveiling the Science

Salt, primarily composed of sodium chloride, is fundamental to life. It regulates fluid balance, aids nerve function, and contributes to muscular contractions. However, the common misconception that salt is universally harmful oversimplifies a more intricate reality that ignores the already demonstrated fact that not all salts are the same in their composition.

Fact vs. Fiction

The narrative often overspills with absolutes—too much salt is disastrous, none is saintly. The reality, however, lies in the shades of grey. Excessive salt intake (particularly table salt and other salt variants that are loaded with anti-caking agents and other additives) is associated with health risks, including elevated blood pressure and increased cardiovascular strain. Nevertheless, the relationship isn't uniform for everyone. Some individuals are more sensitive to salt's impact, while others handle it with ease.

Understanding the Nuances

Navigating the labyrinth of salt's health impact requires understanding the nuances. Moderation emerges as the beacon in this maze. The right balance—neither too little nor too much—is the key. While reducing salt intake benefits some, drastic cuts can be counterproductive for others. Mineral rich salts such as those described in the preceding chapter should always be considered as more favourable and less harmful than the common highly processed table salt.

The Complexity of Moderation

The idea is not to eliminate salt entirely but to find the balance that best suits individual needs. It's about understanding how much salt an individual's body requires without tipping the scales towards risk. It's also about acknowledging the role of processed foods, which contribute significantly to overall salt intake, and the necessity of conscientious choices in everyday diet.

The discourse surrounding salt's impact on health is neither a saga of absolute truths nor a tapestry of absolute myths. It's a complex narrative—interweaving science, individuality, and moderation. It calls for a nuanced approach, understanding that health is as diverse as the individuals it encompasses.

The Delicate Dance of Flavor and Health: Mastering Salt in Culinary Art

In the captivating world of culinary finesse, the symphony of flavours unfolds in a delicate balance between taste and well-being.

To master this art is to navigate the seas of seasoning, discovering the secrets that honour taste while safeguarding health.

Harmony in Seasoning

Salt, the maestro of taste, needs not always take the centre stage. Crafting flavourful dishes without an overwhelming sodium footprint demands the finesse of balance. The secret lies in the harmonious interplay of various seasonings, herbs, and culinary techniques.

Reducing salt without compromising taste is an art in itself. Techniques like layering flavours with aromatic herbs, spices, and citrus zest create depth without relying solely on salt. Slowly infusing flavours through marinating, braising, and slow-cooking allows ingredients to impart richness without the need for excessive salt.

Substitutions and Seasoning Strategies

The canvas of culinary mastery welcomes the use of substitutes like garlic, onions, and vinegars, imparting a tangy touch without overwhelming the palate with salt. Utilising umami-rich ingredients such as mushrooms or tomatoes adds depth, creating a savoury experience that mitigates the need for excessive salt.

Crafting Healthy Equilibrium

Embracing alternative seasonings, from smoky paprika to zesty lemon zest, opens a world of possibilities. These additions not only elevate flavours but also offer a healthier equilibrium, granting a vibrant spectrum of taste without compromising on well-being.

In conclusion, the essence of this culinary journey lies in the revelation that taste need not be sacrificed for health. It's a celebration of creativity, an exploration of tastes, an ode to the craft of seasoning. It's a journey where the delicate balance of flavours harmonises with the pursuit of well-being.

Sources:

Bitterman, Mark. "Salted: A Manifesto on the World's Most Essential Mineral." Ten Speed Press, 2010.
Food and Nutrition Board, Institute of Medicine. "Dietary Reference Intakes for Water, Potassium, Sodium, Chloride, and Sulfate." National Academies Press, 2005.
Kurlansky, Mark. "Salt: A World History." Penguin Books, 2003.
Mayo Clinic. "Reducing salt in your diet." 2021.
Dietary Guidelines for Americans. U.S. Department of Health and Human Services, 2020-2025.
National Institutes of Health. "Sodium and Salt." MedlinePlus, 2021.
Stein, L.J., Cowart, B.J., & Beauchamp, G.K. "The development of salty taste acceptance is related to dietary experience in human infants: a prospective study." The American Journal of Clinical Nutrition, 2012.
Strazzullo, P., D'Elia, L., & Kandala, N.B. "Salt intake, stroke, and cardiovascular disease: meta-analysis of prospective studies." BMJ, 2009.
Truffle, Carlo, et al. "The Taste of Salt." Culinary Institute of America, 2015.

VII: Culinary Alchemy with Salts

Salt is more than just a mere seasoning; it's the sorcerer's wand in the realm of flavour. Its versatility isn't confined to simply adding saltiness, but it unlocks the door to a treasure trove of tastes, transforming ordinary dishes into extraordinary culinary delights.

Enhancing Flavours with Salt

Salts aren't one-size-fits-all; they're the magicians in a symphony of flavours. Each salt brings a unique tale to the table. Kosher salt, with its larger grains, is the reliable friend in brining, seasoning, or curing meats. Sea salt, harvested from ocean waters, adds a subtle crunch and oceanic essence to seafood and salads, while fleur de sel delicately crowns dishes as a finishing touch. Understanding these distinctions is the first step in wielding salt's magical power.

Crafting Gastronomic Wonders

Recipes that dance with the essence of different salts elevate the culinary experience. Take, for instance, a delectable Fleur de Sel caramel: a seductive blend of sweet and salty that transcends the ordinary. Or perhaps, a

Himalayan salt-crusted fish that weaves a tale of tradition and innovation, infusing the fish with a subtle pink hue and a nuanced taste. The harmony of a simple Caprese salad comes alive with a sprinkle of artisanal salts, enhancing the flavours without overpowering the dish.

The Art of Seasoning: Tips and Tricks

Incorporating various salts into your culinary repertoire isn't just a choice; it's a craft. For an enchanting barbecue rub, experiment with smoked salt to introduce an element of smokiness. Infused salts, a blend of salt with herbs or spices, add a whole new dimension to a dish. A pinch of black lava salt atop chocolate desserts elevates the richness. The key is to experiment, explore, and let your taste buds guide the journey.

Indeed the world of salts isn't merely about sodium; it's a kaleidoscope of tastes, a playground of possibilities. The true essence lies in the adventure of blending, sprinkling, and discovering the magic in the mundane. Every dish is a canvas, and salt, the versatile brush that paints the masterpiece.

Sources:

Bitterman, Mark. "Salted: A Manifesto on the World's Most Essential Mineral, with Recipes." Ten Speed Press, 2010.

Ruhlman, Michael. "The Elements of Cooking: Translating the Chef's Craft for Every Kitchen." Scribner, 2007.

Cressy, Thomas. "The Importance of Being Smoky: The World of Smoked Salts." HarperCollins, 2022.

VIII: The Salt Revolution

As the sun sets on the horizon of tradition, a new dawn emerges – the future of salt. The culinary universe, once bound by the familiarity of salt's ancient traditions, now stands at the brink of an extraordinary transformation.

The Evolution of Salt Production

Innovations in salt production have cast a new light upon this age-old mineral. From advanced harvesting methods in salt pans to state-of-the-art technologies in salt extraction, the journey of salt from the sea, mines, and even labs has seen a renaissance. Techniques such as vacuum evaporation and solar desalination now offer salts with distinct mineral compositions and enhanced purity. These innovative methods redefine the narrative of what salt can offer, elevating the art of seasoning.

Potential Impact on Culinary Frontiers

The impact of these advancements resonates across the culinary landscape. The advent of novel salts—be it smoked, infused, or mineral-rich varieties—ushers in a new era of flavours. These salts aren't just condiments; they're ingredients that paint a vibrant tapestry of taste, transforming dishes into culinary marvels. The delicate mineral nuances and textures now play a vital role in a chef's repertoire, inviting new culinary adventures.

The Emergence of Culinary Trends

The future of salt is an ever-evolving saga. It's not just about sprinkling, but a complete sensory experience. The surge of interest in artisanal salts and the growing curiosity in global salt varieties signify an era of exploration. Salts from unique locales, each with its own distinct character, invite chefs and enthusiasts to delve into uncharted territories. The marriage of tradition and innovation crafts a future where salt isn't just a mere seasoning but a passport to uncharted flavour territories.

Embracing the Salt Renaissance

The future of salt isn't merely about taste; it's a revelation of possibilities. It's an evolution that transcends the boundaries of seasoning, offering a journey that unfolds a myriad of culinary adventures. It's a tale where tradition meets technology, and innovation becomes the key that unlocks the doors to a brave new culinary world.

Sources:

Kurlansky, Mark. "Salt: A World History." Penguin Books, 2003.
Food Navigator. "The future of salt: What are the alternatives?" 2022.
National Geographic. "Salt, a potential renewable energy source." 2019.

IX: Salt's Culinary Odyssey

In the grand tapestry of culinary creation, salt stands as the unassuming yet pivotal thread weaving together flavours, tradition, and innovation. This journey through the diverse realm of salts is not merely about taste but an invitation to embark on an extraordinary adventure, transcending the ordinary in your very own kitchen.

The Mosaic of Salts: A Culinary Kaleidoscope

Salt isn't just about sodium chloride; it's a palette of possibilities. From the common table salt to the exotic fleur de sel, each variety tells a story—a story of origin, texture, and flavour. Their diversity isn't just a mere choice but a gateway to an array of tastes waiting to be discovered. They form the cornerstone of culinary heritage, offering an expansive palette to every aspiring chef and enthusiastic home cook.

Importance in the Culinary World

The importance of salt goes beyond seasoning. It's the secret ingredient that transforms mundane dishes into memorable experiences. Its ability to elevate flavours without overshadowing other elements is a testament to its significance. From preserving food to enhancing taste, salt is the silent hero that marries all the flavours on a plate, binding them into a harmonious symphony.

Embrace the Adventure: Your Culinary Canvas

The call to action is simple—embrace the adventure. Dive into the world of salts, experiment, and explore. Venture beyond the conventional; let your taste buds be your guide. From experimenting with various salts in your marinades to discovering the subtleties of finishing a dish with a sprinkle of a specialty salt, the canvas is yours. Unleash your inner chef and paint your culinary masterpiece.

Conclusion: A Salty Farewell

As we bid adieu to this flavorful journey, let us not bid farewell to the discovery and exploration. The culinary world is a vast ocean of tastes, and salt, the compass that navigates this delightful journey. May your culinary escapades be flavoured with the essence of curiosity, exploration, and the gentle touch of diverse salts, as you paint your culinary saga.

Sources:

Bitterman, Mark. "Salted: A Manifesto on the World's Most Essential Mineral, with Recipes." Ten Speed Press, 2010.
Ruhlman, Michael. "The Elements of Cooking: Translating the Chef's Craft for Every Kitchen." Scribner, 2007.
Cressy, Thomas. "The Importance of Being Smoky: The World of Smoked Salts." HarperCollins, 2022.